Hollywood
HORSES

by Meish Goldish

Consultant: Thomas Leitch
University of Delaware

Bearport PUBLISHING

New York, New York

Credits

Cover and Title Page, © Warner Brothers/courtesy, Everett Collection; 4, © Bob Birchard; 5, © Photofest; 6, © Library of Congress Prints and Photographs Division; 7, © Mary Evans Picture Library/Everett Collection; 8, © CSU Archives/Everett Collection; 9, © Photo restoration by Howard and Jill Levine, CDS PhotoGraphics, ©2004 by The Autry Qualified Interest Trust and the Autry Foundation.; 10, © Everett Collection; 11, © CSU Archives/Everett Collection; 12, © Everett Collection; 13, © Everett Collection; 14, © United Artists/The Kobal Collection; 15, © Touchstone/Photofest; 16, © 20th Century-Fox/Photofest; 17, © 20th Century Fox Film Corp. All rights reserved./Courtesy Everett Collection; 18, © American Humane Film and Television Unit; 19, © Touchstone/The Kobal Collection; 20, © DreamWorks/SKG Productions/The Kobal Collection, Joseph Lederer; 21, © DreamWorks/Courtesy Everett Collection; 22, © MGM/Courtesy Everett Collection; 23, © MGM/Courtesy Everett Collection; 24, © Universal/Courtesy Everett Collection; 25, © Universal/The Kobal Collection; 26, © Bettmann/CORBIS; 27, © 20th Century Fox Film Corp. All rights reserved./Courtesy Everett Collection; 28, © Everett Collection; 29A, © Bob Langrish; 29B, © Bob Langrish; 29C, © Bob Langrish; 29D, © Bob Langrish; 29E, © Robert Maier/Animals Animals-Earth Scenes.

Publisher: Kenn Goin
Senior Editor: Lisa Wiseman
Creative Director: Spencer Brinker
Photo Researcher: Amy Dunleavy
Original Design: Stacey May

Library of Congress Cataloging-in-Publication Data

Goldish, Meish.
 Hollywood horses / by Meish Goldish.
   p. cm. — (Horse power)
 Includes bibliographical references and index.
 ISBN-13: 978-1-59716-627-0 (lib. bd.)
 ISBN-10: 1-59716-627-8 (lib. bd.)
 1. Horses in motion pictures. I. Title.

PN1995.9.A5G65 2008
791.43'66296655—dc22

                        2007030469

For more information, write to Bearport Publishing Company, Inc., 101 Fifth Avenue, Suite 6R, New York, New York 10003. Printed in the United States of America.

10 9 8 7 6 5 4 3 2 1

Contents

Horse Actors

William S. Hart was in trouble. The actor was on a movie set riding his horse, Fritz, when the animal slipped. Both Hart and Fritz crashed to the ground. Hart lay trapped under the 1,000-pound (454-kg) horse. Fritz's **hooves** were just inches from Hart's head. If Fritz moved, he might hit Hart in the head, killing him. Luckily, Fritz lay still until help arrived.

William S. Hart and Fritz were the first cowboy-and-horse team in Hollywood.

In the early 1900s, Fritz starred in many **silent movies** with Hart. Fritz wasn't a pet. He was a talented actor. He could jump through windows and leap over fire.

Hart called Fritz "the greatest all-around horse that ever lived."

Fritz even had his own fans. They wrote him letters and sent him his favorite treat—sugar cubes.

Picture Perfect

Horses have always played an important role in Hollywood. In fact, movies were invented because of them. In the 1870s, a California horse owner named Leland Stanford made a bet with a friend. Stanford believed that when a horse runs, all four feet come off the ground at some point. He hired a photographer to prove it.

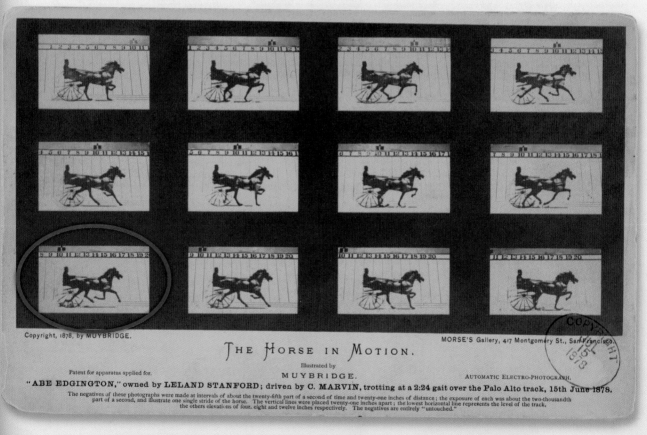

Copyright, 1878, by MUYBRIDGE.

MORSE'S Gallery, 417 Montgomery St., San Francisco.

THE HORSE IN MOTION.

Illustrated by

Patent for apparatus applied for. MUYBRIDGE.

AUTOMATIC ELECTRO-PHOTOGRAPH.

"ABE EDGINGTON," owned by LELAND STANFORD; driven by C. MARVIN, trotting at a 2:24 gait over the Palo Alto track, 15th June 1878.

The negatives of these photographs were made at intervals of about the twenty-fifth part of a second of time and twenty-one inches of distance; the exposure of each was about the two-thousandth part of a second, and illustrate one single stride of the horse. The vertical lines were placed twenty-one inches apart; the lowest horizontal line represents the level of the track, the others elevations of four, eight and twelve inches respectively. The negatives are entirely "untouched."

These pictures are part of a series that prove a horse lifts all his feet in the air for a split second when he runs. The photo circled in red shows the horse with all his feet off the ground.

Twelve cameras were placed in a line. They snapped photos of a horse as he ran by. The pictures were all taken in just half a second. They not only proved that Stanford was right, but this type of photography led to the creation of the **motion picture**.

In 1889, inventor Thomas Edison developed the first movie camera.

Thomas Edison

A True Champion

In the 1930s, Hollywood was making **talking pictures**. Many of them starred a singing cowboy named Gene Autry and his horse, Champion. Together, they made 91 **Westerns**.

Champion, a **sorrel**, could do many tricks. He could dance the hula. He could jump through a ring of fire. He could even roll over and play dead.

Champion takes a bow.

Champion became so popular that in the 1950s he starred in his own TV show without Gene Autry.

Champion became a big star. In 1940, he was the first horse to fly across the United States on an airplane. Five rows of seats were taken out of the plane to make room for his **stall**. He ate carrots during the takeoff and the landing. The chewing kept his ears from hurting when the **air pressure** in the plane changed.

Champion traveled to many places around the world to take part in special shows with Gene Autry.

Teaming Up

The success of Gene Autry and Champion led to more cowboy-and-horse teams. One of the most popular was Roy Rogers and Trigger. Trigger was a golden **palomino**. He was fast, strong, and very talented. In one film, Trigger chased a speeding truck. Large barrels rolled off the truck's back. Trigger leaped over them easily. The scene was filmed without a single **rehearsal**!

Trigger was famous for rising up high on his back legs.

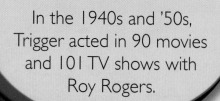

In the 1940s and '50s, Trigger acted in 90 movies and 101 TV shows with Roy Rogers.

Later, Rogers made movies with Dale Evans. She rode a **quarter horse** named Buttermilk. Her horse was even faster than Trigger. In chase scenes, Evans had to hold back Buttermilk so Trigger could keep up.

Rogers and Evans married. In the 1950s, they had their own TV show. Of course, Trigger and Buttermilk starred in it, too!

Dale Evans named her horse Buttermilk because of his white color.

A Talking Horse

Horses acted in other shows besides Westerns. In the 1960s, a TV **sitcom** starred a talking horse named Mister Ed. Of course, the palomino could not really speak. An unseen actor spoke the horse's lines as Mister Ed's mouth moved. On screen, it looked as if the horse was talking.

On the show, Mister Ed could "read" as well as "speak."

A **trainer** named Les Hilton made Mister Ed "talk." He ran a soft string under the horse's upper lip. Whenever the actor spoke, Hilton gently tugged on the string from offstage, making the horse's mouth move.

Mister Ed learned many **stunts**. He could dial a telephone. He could hit a baseball with a bat. He could even drive a truck!

Many fans thought Mister Ed was fed peanut butter to get him to move his lips as if he was talking.

Mister Ed also enjoyed playing chess.

Special Training

Trainers such as Les Hilton teach animals amazing stunts. For example, some horses learn to fall safely while running. To teach this stunt, a trainer stands by the horse and gently pulls the animal to the ground. This move is practiced day after day. After the horse is comfortable doing this, he learns to fall with a rider on his back.

Before a fall, the trainer makes sure the ground is soft so that the horse doesn't get hurt.

Many movie horses are trained without the use of **reins**. Instead, they learn to follow the hand signals of their trainer.

Some horses also learn to lie still once they have fallen. In the movie *The Red Pony* (1949), the horse hero dies. Birds come to eat his skin. For the film, a pony was trained to play dead. Pieces of meat were placed on him. The animal had to be still as birds picked at the food. Now that's talent!

A trainer works with a horse on the set of the movie *The Horse Whisperer* (1998).

Tricks

Even with well-trained horses, Hollywood directors often use tricks of their own when filming. In the movie *My Friend Flicka* (1943), the star horse is caught in **barbed wire**. The wire was not dangerous, however, because it was made of rubber. Fake blood was spread on the horse. The scene looked so real that many viewers wrote angry letters to the movie studio.

In *My Friend Flicka*, the horse didn't really get hurt. She was just acting.

Flicka (2006) was a **remake** of the 1943 film. In this movie, the director also used tricks. In one scene, a horse kicked a character in the shoulder. A fake hoof was used for the stunt. The actress in the scene was a trained stunt person. Both the horse and the actress were safe at all times.

 In movies, fake glass called "candy glass" is used. It is safe to break and won't harm the horse or the other actors.

Actors Alison Lohman and Tim McGraw and their horses work with the director of the movie *Flicka*.

Playing It Safe

Years ago, animal actors often got hurt on the job. Today, the American Humane Association (AHA) protects these animals. Before filming starts, AHA workers read the **script**. They carefully plan scenes with the director. They make sure all stunts are rehearsed so that the horses stay safe. Then they watch the filming to make certain that the animals are never in danger.

On the set of *The Chronicles of Narnia: Prince Caspian* (2008), an AHA rep makes sure that Civilon, a horse actor, stays safe.

At the end of a movie that the AHA has worked on, they state that no animals were harmed during the making of the film.

In *Hidalgo* (2004), the horse hero must fight two leopards. For safety, the animals were filmed separately. First, the leopards growled and swung their claws for the camera. After they were led away, the horse came on the set. He attacked fake leopards. Later, the two films were pieced together. On screen, it looked as if the leopards and horse were really fighting each other.

Before horses run, workers from the AHA check the path for rocks, holes, and branches to make sure the animals don't trip and fall.

Horses and Children

Actors must be careful when working with horses. Child actors must be extra careful. Dakota Fanning was 11 years old when she starred in the movie *Dreamer* (2005). She had never ridden a horse before. She spent six weeks working with the animals and a trainer. Fanning learned quickly. "It was really exciting and really fun," she said.

Fanning learned a lot about horses while making the movie *Dreamer*.

In one scene, Fanning had to ride a wild horse without wearing a helmet. A real horse would have been too dangerous for her. So she rode a **mechanical** horse instead. Movie viewers couldn't tell the difference. On screen, the fake horse looked very real!

A fake horse used in a movie or TV show is called a **stuffie**.

A scene from *Dreamer* being filmed with the fake horse

Seeing Double

Audiences can often be fooled when watching horses in a movie. Some horse stars have **doubles**. A double replaces the star when extra-special talent is needed.

In *The Black **Stallion*** (1979), a horse named Cass Olé won the lead part. Five horses served as doubles. They played the stallion in scenes that involved fighting, running, and swimming.

Cass Olé had a lot of talent. It didn't take much work to train him.

Two doubles were hired for the swimming scenes. The horses did not look like Cass Olé. They were white, not black. The problem, however, was solved quickly. A safe color **dye** was used on the horses. After filming, the dye washed off easily with soap.

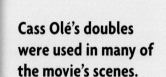

Cass Olé's doubles were used in many of the movie's scenes.

The movie *The Black Stallion* was based on a popular book of the same title by Walter Farley.

And They're Off!

Making a movie with many horses can be a challenge. More than 40 horses were used in *Seabiscuit* (2003). The film is about a racehorse that recovers from an injury and becomes a champion. Many horses were used in the race scenes. Nine horses served as doubles for the star.

One of the horses that played Seabiscuit in a scene with his human costars

Training 40 horses was a big job. Work started six weeks before the movie began shooting. The animals learned to follow a camera as it moved. They were taught to stand still with microphones above their heads. Real-life **jockeys** were used in the racing scenes. They controlled the horses' speed so the right horse won each race.

The movie *Seabiscuit* is based on a true story. The real Seabiscuit lived more than 60 years ago.

The racing scenes in *Seabiscuit* used trained horses and jockeys.

And the Winner Is . . .

Horses and many other animals have starred in movies and TV shows. In the past, PATSY Awards were given to the best animal actors. Trigger won a PATSY Award in 1953 and 1958. Mister Ed won a PATSY four years in a row, from 1962 to 1965.

Mister Ed receiving his second PATSY award in 1963

The American Humane Association created the PATSY Awards.

Today, horses still appear in movies and on TV. Few of them become big stars. Like all actors, they need talent and luck to succeed. Yet horses have always thrilled audiences. They have entertained since the earliest silent movies. They will continue to win the hearts of viewers in the future.

Just the Facts

- The first Hollywood Western which featured horses was *The Great Train Robbery* (1903). It was only 12 minutes long.

- Over the years, many different horses played the part of Champion in Gene Autry's movies, TV shows, and personal appearances.

- When Trigger and Buttermilk died, Roy Rogers did not want to bury them. Instead, he saved their bodies by having them stuffed. Today, both horses can be seen at the Roy Rogers–Dale Evans Museum in Branson, Missouri.

- Mister Ed had a double named Pumpkin. Mister Ed was very jealous of him. If visitors on the set said hello to Pumpkin first, Mister Ed would get upset and walk away.

- The American Humane Association began to protect animal actors after a horse was run off a cliff and killed during the filming of a movie in 1939.

- One of the best-known horses in the 1950s was a white stallion named Silver. He starred in a TV show called *The Lone Ranger*. Fans loved to hear the Lone Ranger cry, "Hi-yo, Silver, away!" as they rode off together.

Common Breeds

Hollywood Horses

Arabian

Tennessee
Walking Horse

Quarter Horse

American Saddlebred

Thoroughbred

Glossary

air pressure (AIR PRESH-ur) the weight of the air, which is greater near the Earth than it is high in the sky

barbed wire (BARBD WIRE) wire with small, sharp points used for fences

doubles (DUH-buhlz) actors who stand in for other actors in scenes where special talent is needed

dye (DYE) a chemical or substance used to change the color of something

hooves (HUVS) the hard coverings on the feet of a horse

jockeys (JAHK-eez) people who ride horses in a race

mechanical (muh-KAN-uh-kuhl) run by a machine

motion picture (MOH-shuhn PIK-chur) a movie

palomino (*pal*-uh-MEE-noh) a golden-tan or cream-colored horse with a white mane and tail

quarter horse (KWOR-tur HORSS) a breed of horse that can run at full speed for a quarter of a mile

rehearsal (ri-HURSS-uhl) practice for a performance

reins (RAYNZ) straps used to control or guide a horse

remake (REE-mayk) a movie that is a newer version of the original one

script (SKRIPT) the written text of a movie, play, or TV show

silent movies (SYE-luhnt MOO-veez) early movies that had no sound

sitcom (SIT-*kom*) a funny TV show that features the same group of characters each week

sorrel (SOR-uhl) a reddish-brown-colored horse, often with a mane and tail of a lighter color

stall (STAWL) an area where an animal is kept

stallion (STAL-yuhn) an adult male horse

stuffie (STUHF-ee) a fake animal that is used in place of a real one in a movie or TV show

stunts (STUHNTS) tricks and dangerous acts that take skill and bravery to perform

talking pictures (TAWK-ing PIK-churz) movies with sound

trainer (TRAY-nur) a person who teaches animals tricks

Westerns (WESS-turnz) cowboy movies or TV shows set in the western part of the United States

Bibliography

Beck, Ken, and Jim Clark. *The Encyclopedia of TV Pets: A Complete History of Television's Greatest Animal Stars.* Nashville, TN: Rutledge Hill Press (2002).

Hintz, H. F. *Horses in the Movies.* Cranbury, NJ: A. S. Barnes (1979).

Mitchum, Petrine Day. *Hollywood Hoofbeats: Trails Blazed Across the Silver Screen.* Irvine, CA: Bow Tie Press (2005).

Read More

Crisp, Marty. *Everything Horse: What Kids Really Want to Know About Horses.* Minnetonka, MN: NorthWord (2005).

Gaff, Jackie. *I Wonder Why Horses Wear Shoes: And Other Questions About Horses.* Boston: Houghton Mifflin (2002).

Holub, Joan. *Why Do Horses Neigh?* New York: Puffin Books (2003).

Saville, Lynn. *Horses in the Circus Ring.* New York: Dutton (1989).

Van Der Linde, Laurel. *From Mustangs to Movie Stars: Five True Horse Legends of Our Time.* Minneapolis, MN: Millbrook Press (1995).

Learn More Online

To learn more about Hollywood horses, visit
www.bearportpublishing.com/HorsePower

Index

About the Author

Meish Goldish has written more than 100 books for children.
In his free time, he likes to horse around.